Impact of
the Holocaust

Titles in The Holocaust in History *Series*

Impact of the Holocaust

Linda Jacobs Altman

Enslow Publishers, Inc.

40 Industrial Road   PO Box 38
Box 398   Aldershot
Berkeley Heights, NJ 07922   Hants GU12 6BP
USA   UK

http://www.enslow.com

Library of Congress Cataloging-in-Publication Data

Altman, Linda Jacobs, 1943–

    Impact of the Holocaust / Linda Jacobs Altman.
      p. cm. — (The Holocaust in history)
    Summary: Discusses the effects and legacy of the Holocaust, including the experiences of survivors, the urgency to establish a Jewish homeland in Palestine, the need for a worldwide human rights policy, and the need to examine the terrible cost of racism and hatred.
    Includes bibliographical references and index.
    ISBN 0-7660-1996-9
    1. Holocaust, Jewish (1939-1945)—Juvenile literature. 2. Holocaust, Jewish (1939-1945)—Influence—Juvenile literature. 3. Holocaust survivors—Juvenile literature. 4. Jews—History—1945—-Juvenile literature. [1. Holocaust, Jewish (1939-1945) 2. Holocaust, Jewish (1939-1945)—Influence. 3. Holocaust survivors. 4. Jews—History—1945-] I. Title. II. Series.
D804.34.A494   2004
341.4'8—dc22

                                   2003021118

Illustration Credits: Ann Byers, p. 12; © Corel Corporation, p. 25; Courtesy of the Simon Wiesenthal Center in Los Angeles, California, pp. 32, 75; Courtesy of Yad Vashem, the Holocaust Martyrs' and Heroes' Remembrance Authority, p. 83; Enslow Publishers, Inc., pp. 8, 19; National Archives and Records Administration, pp. 1, 2, 3, 5, 6, 10, 23, 35, 36, 49, 50, 54, 62, 66; UN/DPI Photo, pp. 21; USHMM, pp. 74, 85, 86, 88; USHMM, courtesy of Alex Hochhauser, p. 14; USHMM, courtesy of Alice Lev, pp. 18, 24; USHMM, courtesy of Amira Kohn-Trattner, p. 17; USHMM, courtesy of Archiwum Panstwowego Muzeum na Majdanku , p. 82; USHMM, courtesy of the Central Zionist Archives, pp. 27, 28; USHMM, courtesy of Hans Pauli, p. 58; USHMM, courtesy of Israel Government Press Office, pp. 52, 64, 69, 70, 72; USHMM, courtesy of Jack Sutin, p. 15; USHMM, courtesy of Jan Kostanski, p. 40; USHMM, courtesy of Jimmy Carter Library, p. 77; USHMM, courtesy of Lawrence E. Gichner, p. 56; USHMM, courtesy of Lidia Kleinman Siciarz, pp. 39, 43; USHMM, courtesy of the National Archives, pp. 79, 84; USHMM, courtesy of Susan Mosheim Alterman, pp. 11, 13; Yad Vashem, pp. 30, 46, 61.

Cover Illustration: National Archives and Records Administration

Contents

Adolf Hitler parades in front of his troops in Nuremberg, Germany, on November 9, 1935.

Introduction
World War II and the Holocaust

On September 1, 1939, German troops invaded Poland. Two days later, Britain and France declared war on Germany. World War II had begun. Under Adolf Hitler and his National Socialist German Workers' Party, also called the Nazi party, Germany would soon conquer most of Europe.

Hitler planned to build a *Reich*, or empire, that would last for a thousand years. He believed that Northern Europeans, or Aryans as he called them, were a master race—a group of people superior to others.

Hitler falsely believed that some people, such as Jews, homosexuals, Gypsies, Poles, Russians, and people of color, were inferior. These people would be given no rights in his Reich. Some would be exterminated, or killed. Others would be kept alive only so long as they served their Aryan masters. It was a dark and terrible vision that cost millions of lives.

In the early days of the war, Germany seemed unbeatable. One nation after another fell to the German *blitzkrieg*, or "lightning war." The Nazis conquered Poland in just twenty-six days. Denmark, Norway, Belgium, the Netherlands, and France fell in the spring of 1940.

By the end of 1940, the Germans had occupied most of Western Europe and made alliances with Italy and Japan. The Axis, as this alliance was called, soon conquered

By the end of 1940, the German army had occupied most of Western Europe, including Poland, Austria, Denmark, Norway, France, Belgium, and the Netherlands.

parts of Asia, Eastern Europe, and North Africa.

In 1941, the picture changed. In June, Germany invaded the Soviet Union, now called Russia. America entered the war on December 7, after Japan attacked the U.S. naval base in Pearl Harbor, Hawaii. The Germans soon found themselves fighting the British and the Americans in the West, and the Soviets in the East. They also devoted men and resources to exterminating Jews and other people the Nazis saw as inferior.

Even when the war turned against Germany, this slaughter did not stop. Trains that could have carried troops and supplies to the fighting fronts were used instead to transport victims to death camps. The killing continued until the last possible moment.

After Germany surrendered on May 7, 1945, survivors began telling what they had suffered. Pictures of starving prisoners, mass graves, and gas chambers disguised as showers appeared in newspapers and movie newsreels. People all over the world were horrified.

As survivors told their stories, the horror grew. New words came into the language. Old words took on new meanings. *Holocaust* came to represent mass murder on a scale that had never been seen before. *Genocide*

American officers and soldiers discovered many dead bodies at the Nazi concentration camps. Here, General Dwight D. Eisenhower (center, wearing hat with hands on hips) and other military men view some of the many killed at Ohrdruf Camp in Germany.

described the systematic killing of specific racial or ethnic groups.

These words are reminders of a grim truth—human beings can do terrible things to one another. This is why knowledge about the Holocaust is so important. It is the best defense against the hatred that produced the Nazi racist state and caused the death of innocent millions.

"Never Again!"

"Never again!" After the Holocaust, this slogan became the rallying cry of Jews. It is a vow to resist oppression, and a warning that Jews will never again go as quietly to the slaughter. They will fight back, however strong the enemy, however hopeless the battle. It is also a pledge to defend human rights everywhere and for everyone.

The Holocaust forever changed the world for survivors. Millions found their homes destroyed, their families dead. They had no place to go.

The effect of the Holocaust gave new urgency to the Jewish quest for a homeland in Palestine in the Middle East. It focused attention on the need for a strong, worldwide human rights policy. Most of all, it forced people to deal with the reality of human evil.

The words "Never Again" appear on a monument outside the Dachau Memorial Museum. (Dachau was a concentration camp during World War II.) The words appear in four languages from top to bottom: French, English, German, and Russian.

Palestine and the Jews

The Jewish longing for Palestine dated from A.D. 70. According to their religious tradition, Jews belonged in Palestine because God himself chose it for them.

The modern dream of a Jewish state began with journalist Theodor Herzl. On February 14, 1896, he published a book: *The Jewish State*. It started a movement that became known as

Zionism, named after Mount Zion in Palestine's Jerusalem. To devout Jews, Zion symbolized a spiritual homeland.

Zionism began with the idea that the Jewish people were a nation without a homeland. They had become a permanent minority group, scattered over many countries. Wherever they went, they became outsiders who never fully belonged to the dominant culture. That made them easy targets for suspicion and hatred. Herzl did not believe this would change: "We are a *people*—*one* people.

For hundreds of years, Jewish people did not have a homeland. From 1939 to 1940, these men fled from Germany and Austria. They had this picture taken at Kitchner refugee camp in Richborough, England.

In 1949, children in Munich, Germany, commemorate the forty-fifth anniversary of Theodor Herzl's death.

We have sincerely tried everywhere to merge with the national communities in which we live, seeking only to preserve the faith of our fathers. It is not permitted us."[1]

Herzl promoted Zionism with zeal and passion. As the movement grew, European Jews began settling in Palestine. These early immigrants came as pioneers. They wanted to belong in this ancient home of their ancestors. They wanted to build, to plant, to reclaim the land. These newcomers faced hardships, but they also found satisfaction in the task before them.

The Holocaust survivors did not come as pioneers, but as refugees. To go to Palestine, they had to cope with the terrors of their past and the barriers of their present. The Yishuv, or Jewish community in Palestine, stood ready to take them. But the British, who governed the region, restricted immigration.

Jewish refugees at the Landsberg, Germany, displaced persons camp demonstrate against Britain's stance on immigration to Palestine.

They did this to keep peace with local Arabs, followers of Islam.

The Birth of Israel

In the Jewish settlements of Palestine and the displaced persons (DP) camps of Europe, Jews fought these restrictions. They built a large organization to smuggle refugees from the camps to the Yishuv. In Palestine, Jewish commando units attacked British installations. It was a dark and violent time. The situation became so difficult that the United Nations (UN) got involved.

On November 29, 1947, the General Assembly passed Resolution 181. It called for the partition of Palestine into two states: one Jewish and one Arab. The resolution set boundaries for both new nations and developed a plan for ending British rule.

Throughout Palestine and the world, Jews celebrated. They began preparing for a new Jewish State. In a 1944 speech, future Israeli prime minister David Ben-Gurion had called that state "the consummation [completion] of the Jewish revolution."[2]

British rule ended at midnight on May 14, 1948. Jewish leaders promptly declared independence. The new State of Israel became a free and sovereign nation.

Some Jews immigrated to Palestine before the nation of Israel was even created. Ruth Kohn and her daughter Rena took a ship to Palestine in 1938.

Prior to the establishment of Israel, David Ben-Gurion delivers a speech at the Zeilsheim, Germany, displaced persons camp in 1946.

It also became a nation at war. Israel's Arab neighbors refused to accept the Jewish state. On May 15, the armies of Egypt, Jordan, Iraq, and Syria attacked. The Israelis fought back with surprising strength.

The war of independence continued through February 1949. The Israelis conquered most of the territory set aside for an Arab state—and they meant to keep it. Israel claimed that the Arab attack had voided, or canceled, the boundaries set by the United Nations.

The end of the war left the Jewish state fairly secure. The Arab state did not exist.

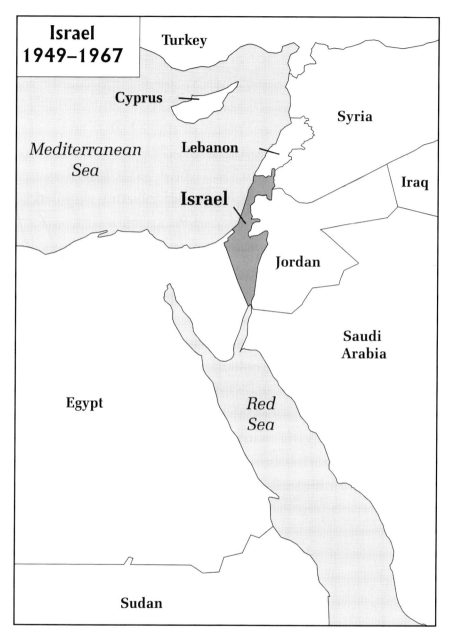

Israel 1949–1967

Turkey

Cyprus

Mediterranean Sea

Lebanon

Syria

Iraq

Israel

Jordan

Saudi Arabia

Egypt

Red Sea

Sudan

Israel maintained the above borders until the Six-Day War in 1967, when Israel gained more land.

Thousands of Palestinian Arabs fled their homes, fearful of Jewish rule. Many ended up in refugee camps in Jordan, Syria, Lebanon, and the Egyptian Gaza Strip. Thus began a conflict that would last into the twenty-first century.

The Holocaust and International Law

The plight of European Jews raised broader issues about human rights. Many people believe that no government can lawfully take away these rights. Every human being possesses them from birth.

The American Declaration of Independence listed these rights as "life, liberty, and the pursuit of happiness."[3] In his famous "Four Freedoms" speech of 1941, President Franklin D. Roosevelt cited freedom of speech and freedom of worship, along with freedom from want and freedom from fear.

The founders of the United Nations considered these ideas when they met to create a new international organization. World War II was not yet over when representatives of fifty nations assembled in San Francisco. On October 24, 1945, they ratified, or approved, a founding document, known as a charter.

The first article called for cooperation "in promoting and encouraging respect for

The first meeting of the UN General Assembly marked the start of new era in international politics.

human rights and for fundamental freedoms for all without distinction as to race, sex, language or religion."[4]

Thus, the charter recognized human rights as an international concern. It provided a basis for United Nations jurisdiction, or authority, in matters of human rights. That alone was an important accomplishment.

Within its own borders, a sovereign, or independent, nation recognizes no authority but its own. There is no "world government" to make and enforce laws that are binding to all nations. Foreign interference is generally regarded as an act of war.

Governments deal with one another by making treaties and alliances. They can band together for a common purpose such as trade or mutual defense. They can also band together to make war.

For example, World War II pitted two alliances against each other. Germany and Japan headed an alliance known as the *Axis*; Great Britain, the United States, and the Soviet Union were known as the *Allies*. Each nation agreed to respect the sovereignty of its partners.

Sovereignty has always been the main stumbling block for international law. Governments refused to surrender authority to an international agency. When the world saw the full horror of the Holocaust, that began to change.

International Justice

In August 1945, the Allied powers created a multinational court to judge Nazi war crimes. In the process, they made history. Never before had the leaders of a nation at war been held to answer for their crimes before an international court.

The International War Crimes Tribunal included judges from the United States, Great Britain, the Soviet Union, and France. They sat in judgment on twenty-two leading Nazis.

Twenty-one of the defendants listen as they are tried by the International War Crimes Tribunal.

With the same spirit of international cooperation, the UN formed the Commission on Human Rights in June 1946. Eleanor Roosevelt, widow of President Franklin Delano Roosevelt, was appointed to lead it.

She faced an enormous task: creating a Universal Declaration of Human Rights. It would apply to all people at all times, regardless of where they lived.

The very idea of a Universal Declaration raised serious issues of national sovereignty. Roosevelt's grasp of those issues kept the commission on track. Even so, the work took almost three years.

Eleanor Roosevelt, a former first lady, visited a memorial to Holocaust victims at the Zeilsheim, Germany, DP camp in 1946.

During that time, the commission saw bloodshed in Palestine and despair in the DP camps of Europe. They saw trials of seemingly ordinary people who had committed unthinkable crimes. They heard from survivors who were scarred for life by their experiences. These things became constant, dark reminders of the need for a strong statement on human rights.

In 1948, the commission ratified, or approved, two historic agreements: the Convention on the Prevention and Punishment of the Crime of Genocide on December 9, and

Eleanor Roosevelt holds the Universal Declaration of Rights, ratified by the UN's Commission on Human Rights.

the Universal Declaration of Human Rights on December 10.

The genocide convention made mass murder of particular groups into an international crime that could be judged and punished under international law. The Universal Declaration of Human Rights identified rights that everyone should possess, simply because they are human beings.

For example, Article 1 states: "All human beings are born free and equal in dignity and rights." These rights were specifically outlined in the following articles. They included freedom of "thought, conscience and religion," as well as freedom of assembly, and the right to own property.[5] Several clauses gave freedom *from* such things as torture, slavery, and arrest without sufficient reason.

The declaration did not have the force of law, but it did have moral authority. It gave hope for a world in which racism, hatred, and genocide would have no place.

Interrupted Lives

Rivka Waxman came to Israel in 1948 as a refugee from Poland. She settled in the city of Haifa. Like most Holocaust survivors, she struggled to adjust to her new life and come to terms with the past. Then a chance meeting brought past and present together.

It happened on a downtown street. Waxman was walking past a movie theater just as a young soldier made his way to the ticket window. Something about him seemed familiar, so she looked more closely.

Suddenly, Waxman stopped in her tracks and shouted out a name: "Haim?" The soldier turned to face her.

A heartbeat later, the two hugged one another; crying and laughing at the same time. Haim was Rivka Waxman's son, separated

Before the nation of Israel was created, refugees could not always settle in Palestine. These British soldiers are removing a boy from a ship that was bound for the area.

from her by the war. For eight years, each thought the other dead.

Most Holocaust refugees were not as lucky as Waxman and her son. Instead of joyous reunions, they faced one loss after another. Many had to adjust to a new country, learn a new language, and work at whatever menial jobs they could find. They had to live with memories that would not fade, scars that would not heal, and guilt that ate away at the soul.

For many survivors, certain memories became personal symbols of the entire Holocaust experience. Often, the incidents themselves were small. For example, Italian writer Primo Levy remembered a melting icicle and a brutal guard. Nazi hunter Simon Wiesenthal remembered a brief meeting with a dying German soldier.

Primo Levy Asks Why

Chemist Primo Levy was twenty-five years old when he became a prisoner in Auschwitz. His unforgettable memory began with an icicle hanging outside his barracks window. Watching it drip made him aware of a painful thirst. He opened the window and held a tin cup under the icicle. He collected water carefully, drop by drop. Then he pulled the cup back inside and lifted it to his lips.

This is how Primo Levy looked before the war.

Before he could drink, a passing guard slapped the cup out of his hands. The water spilled on the floor. "Why?" Levy wailed to the guard in his anguish. The guard replied: "In here there is no why."[1]

To Primo Levy this summed up one of the most difficult parts of concentration camp life: Nothing made sense, or was even supposed to make sense. Looking for meaning in such a place only made the pain worse.

After the war, Primo Levy seemed to recover from his ordeal. He was able to go home to Italy and pick up the threads of his life. He worked as a chemist and wrote books about his experiences in a place where there was no *why*.

For years, he coped with the memories, the meaninglessness, and the guilt. As he grew older, he became distant and distracted. Old age was more than he could bear. Once again, life began to lose its meaning.

Here there is no why, the guard had said. On April 11, 1987, Primo Levy died in a fall that was ruled suicide. He was sixty-seven years old.

Simon Wiesenthal and the Soldier

Simon Wiesenthal's nagging memory began on a work detail. He and other concentration camp prisoners were hauling garbage out of a

German military hospital. Suddenly a nurse rushed up to Wiesenthal and asked if he was a Jew.

Wiesenthal was so startled that he said nothing. The nurse seemed to take his silence as a "yes" and asked him to come with her. She led him to a dim hospital room. There on the bed, a young SS soldier lay dying.

Wiesenthal could not see the young man's face. Afterward, he remembered only "White, bloodless hands on the [coverlet], head completely bandaged with openings only for mouth, nose, and ears."[2]

Simon Wiesenthal (on left, with mustache) celebrated with his wife, Cyla, and friends after World War II.

This Christian soldier wanted to make his final confession, but he had not asked for a priest. He had asked for a Jew.

Wiesenthal was the first Jew the nurse could find. So he found himself listening to the dying man's story.

His SS unit had received orders to wipe out the Jewish population of a small Ukrainian town. The soldiers herded about four hundred men, women, and children into a small wooden house. Then they set the house afire:

> "We heard screams," said the soldier. "We had our rifles ready to shoot down anyone who tried to escape. . . .[3]
>
> "Behind the windows of the second floor, I saw a man with a small child in his arms. His clothes were [on fire]. By his side stood a woman, doubtless the mother of the child. With his free hand the man covered the child's eyes . . . then he jumped into the street. Seconds later the mother followed."[4]

When the soldier finished his story, he asked for forgiveness. Only the forgiveness of a Jew, he believed, could let him die in peace.

Wiesenthal answered with silence. He sat for a moment without speaking. Then he got up and walked quietly out of the room.

The memory of that encounter would haunt Wiesenthal for the rest of his life. Had he done the right thing? The soldier's remorse seemed genuine, yet Wiesenthal answered with silence rather than forgiveness.

Some twenty-five years later, Wiesenthal dealt with the experience in a book. He told the story of the dying soldier and asked religious leaders, human rights activists, and others to comment on his choices.

He collected their responses and his own essay in *The Sunflower: On the Possibilities and Limits of Forgiveness*. This book has become one of the classics of Holocaust literature.

The Walking Wounded

Not all survivors could adjust to freedom. Some remained trapped in the past, its pain and terror defining their lives. Others carried the weight of survivor guilt, endlessly wondering why they had survived while so many others perished.

Another common problem was known as "concentration camp syndrome." Today, that syndrome is included with similar disorders, collectively known as post-traumatic stress disorder (PTSD).

Trauma refers to an injury which may be physical, emotional, or both. People in camps were beaten, terrorized, starved. They saw loved ones marched off to the gas chambers or murdered before their eyes.

Some survivors suffered from post-traumatic stress disorder, due to the horrors they witnessed, beatings they received, and tortures they endured. Above, a survivor points to a guard who severely beat prisoners.

Liberation could not heal the mental and physical scars of those injuries. Some Holocaust survivors developed symptoms of PTSD years after rebuilding their lives. Those symptoms included sleep disturbances, terrifying dreams, memory lapses, painful "flashbacks," and emotional numbing.

A flashback is a memory so vivid it seems to be happening all over again. The sights, the sounds—even the smells—are all there, as terrifying as they were the first time around.

While flashbacks bring strong feelings, emotional numbing does just the opposite. Concentration camp prisoners learned not to feel too deeply. In a place of brutality and death, numbing helped prisoners survive.

Many survivors remained distant and disconnected, long after the threat ended. Emotional blunting had become their

Survivors of the Gotha concentration camp demonstrate how they were tortured by the Nazis, as American general Dwight D. Eisenhower (center, with hands on hips) observes.

"normal" way of relating to the world. They had seen so much death, torture, and horror that they stopped reacting to any of it. Some overcame this blunting; others did not.

For those who did learn to feel again, the way back could be slow and gradual, or it could happen in an instant. For example, writer Anton Gill tells of one survivor who found healing at the funeral service of a beloved aunt:

> [The funeral service] meant nothing to him at all, until . . . he looked at the other mourners and realized that death could be a significant thing: he had come to regard it [as a normal part of daily life] . . . a corpse in the camp meant no more to [prisoners] than litter on a city street means to a pedestrian. But suddenly, this man began to feel like a human being again, and that was a splendid feeling. . . .[5]

Survivor Guilt

Sooner or later, most survivors experienced feelings of guilt. Much of it grew out of a single troublesome question: "Why did I survive when others did not?" Survivors could not always find a satisfying answer to that question.

Hugo Gryn, who became a rabbi after the war, learned to live with his memories, but not with his guilt:

> I have not got over my guilt that I am alive, and I think many [survivors] have that problem.

Rationally, I know that it is not my fault that I survived, but guilt is not always a rational thing. My brother was a much nicer person than me . . . so why isn't he alive, and why am I? And my father was a wonderful man. It is a difficult thing to live with. I can't explain my guilt, but I am always conscious of it. I have tried to [make amends] in my work, but I don't succeed.[6]

Beating Hitler

The senselessness of the Holocaust nagged at survivors. It was one more burden to bear as they tried to rebuild their lives. Many found strength in believing that Jewish survival proved Hitler's failure. Every survivor who lived a rich, full life paid tribute to the millions who were lost. None of this made the memories easier to bear. However, it did give many survivors the courage to go on in spite of those memories.

Childhood Lost

In the Nazi world of ghettos and gas chambers, Jewish children had to grow up quickly. Six- and seven-year-olds risked their lives to smuggle food into the ghettos. Young teenagers worked twelve-hour days on whatever tasks the Nazis gave them.

Children of all ages learned to live by their wits. Many of them became tough, aggressive, and emotionally numb, or unfeeling. In the ghettos and camps, such behavior came to seem almost normal. In the outside world, much of it was unacceptable.

"There was a world of habits to unlearn," said survivor Yehuda Bacon, who spent his early teens in the concentration camps. Bacon remembered the first funeral procession he saw after liberation: "I burst out laughing! People are crazy; for one person they make a casket and play solemn music? A few

These Jewish teenagers helped smuggle necessities into the ghetto in Warsaw, Poland.

weeks ago I saw thousands of bodies piled up to be burnt like so much junk."[1]

Safe Havens

Some children did not have to endure ghettos or camps. They lived in hiding or found safe havens outside of German territory. A program called Kindertransport took Jewish children out of harm's way and sent them to Great Britain. The program operated between December 1938 and the start of the war in September 1939. Within that time, Kindertransport rescued ten thousand Jewish children between the ages of five and seventeen.

The children came from Germany, Czechoslovakia, Austria, and Poland. They went to Great Britain, where they lived with British families or found refuge in institutions such as orphanages and schools.

Though they were physically safe, even the youngest children realized that their lives were not normal. They were homesick and frightened. Some thought their parents had abandoned them to these strangers. Teenagers understood that they had not been abandoned. Still, they could not escape feeling like outsiders—people who did not fully belong to the society in which they found themselves.

Kurt Fuchel became a Kindertransport child in 1939. For him, "temporary" turned out to be a long time. He lived with a Jewish family in England for more than eight years. Looking back as an adult, he talked about how the experience affected his life:

> I became used to "going with the flow" and not affirming myself, so I am not an assertive person. I lack confidence in social situations, and I frequently feel like an outsider, and stand apart. While I was in England, I knew that my parents might someday come and reclaim me, and [so] I have difficulty with making a 100% commitment.[2]

The Hidden Children

Some children who stayed in German territory survived because their parents or other adults put them into hiding. Many hidden children stayed in convents, or communities of Catholic nuns. Others found refuge with gentile families.

In most cases, "hiding" did not mean keeping entirely out of sight. Rescuers gave their children Christian names and false identity papers. They taught them how to behave like Christians. Many a hidden child was saved from discovery because he or she knew when to kneel or how to make the sign of the cross.

Like Kindertransport children, the hidden ones paid a price for their safety. After the war, some children and parents found that living apart for so long had taken a toll on their relationship: "We [parents and child] were like strangers to each other," a former hidden child told psychologist Bloeme Evers-Emden. "It seemed as if I were not welcome at home," said another.[3]

Evers-Emden, who was herself a hidden child, saw this problem many times. In many cases, religion became an issue. Some hidden children had lived as Christians for several years. They knew nothing of Jewish faith and traditions. Many did not want to learn.

Former hidden child William H. Donat remembered being baptized, saying Christian prayers, and going to Mass each Sunday. When his parents took him home, he made fun of Jews and Jewish traditions. He insisted on saying Christian prayers.

Donat resisted his own heritage until the family moved to New York City. There, he slowly began to feel comfortable living with Jewish people in a Jewish neighborhood.

"I consider myself a Jew," he said as an adult. "I married a Jewish girl. We raised our three children to be Jewish. My granddaughter is continuing the tradition."[4]

William Donat did not become religious, but he did honor Jewish culture and tradition. He considered this necessary: "I will not . . . give the [Nazis] a final victory by forsaking

Sister Jadwiga poses with a group of children from a school in Lomma, Poland. The school was run by nuns who helped shelter Jewish children there.

my Jewish identity. Too many died because they were Jews for me to abandon them."[5]

Living With Expectations

Isabella Leitner was a teenager when she went into the camps, and an adult when she came out. She and her two surviving sisters came to live with their father in the United States.

During the war years, Isabella's father found comfort in religion. He became strictly observant of every Jewish law and practice. He wanted his daughters to do the same. He would beg Isabella to go to temple, to pray there for the dead.

In Judaism, the mourner's prayer never mentions death. It is a prayer of praise to God for the miracle of life. Leitner could not make her father understand why she could not speak the words of this ancient prayer.

In her book *Saving the Fragments: From Auschwitz to New York*, she wrote the explanation she never gave him: "the dead didn't just die, Father. They were murdered! I am not grateful for that, Father. My lips freeze in temple. I cannot praise the Lord. I am trying so hard to live with the clutter in my head. Let me be.

"Live the way you can, Father. Let me live the way I can. Please."[6]

Many youthful survivors faced these problems when they returned to the normal world. Those who did have surviving family sometimes found that they could not ease back in to old relationships. The war years had changed them too much for that.

Life on the Run

By the time Alicia Jurman was thirteen, she had lived through Russian and then German occupation of her hometown, Buczaqcz, Poland. Her parents and siblings were dead, and she had nowhere to turn.

She lived on the run, never staying anywhere long enough for people to ask too many questions about her background. Her travels took her through parts of southern Poland and the Ukraine, where she worked the fields in exchange for food. She created new identities for herself as she moved. With Poles, she posed as a Polish peasant girl from a devout Roman Catholic home. With Ukrainians, she spoke Ukrainian and gave herself an Eastern Orthodox background. She even had a different name for each group: Helka with Poles and Slavka with Ukrainians.

When the war ended, Alicia Jurman was still in her teens, and the last survivor of her family. She was used to living on the edge, just a step ahead of disaster. Much as she wanted a normal life, she was not yet ready to settle into one.

She joined a group called the *Brecha* (a Hebrew word that means "to smuggle"). Her job was to guide Jews out of Russian-occupied countries and bring them to safety. The work was both dangerous and illegal, but Alicia did it with iron determination.

Alicia went to Israel after it became an independent nation in May 1948. Even then, she did not settle down; she became a soldier in the Israeli army and fought in the war for independence. In 1949, she met Gabriel

About 1.5 million children did not even survive the Holocaust. These children, along with an elderly woman, are unknowingly on their way to the gas chambers.

Appleman, an American Jew whom she later married. He took her to the United States, where she adapted to yet another culture and yet another language.

Alicia learned to live with her painful memories by sharing them. She became an author and Holocaust lecturer, telling her story in the hope that the lessons of the past could prevent future Holocausts.

Children of Survivors

The shadow of the Holocaust fell over another generation when survivors began having children. Children born to survivors often grew up wondering why their parents were sad and secretive; why they would not talk about the past. Many children sensed that something dark and awful was hidden here.

Journalist Joseph Berger came to the United States with his parents in 1950. Even as a small child, he sensed something different about his family. Later, he learned that his parents were not simply immigrants, coping with a new culture and a new language. They were Holocaust survivors, trying to put painful memories behind them.

Berger noted that being their son was:

> a tangle of experiences. . . . Like other immigrant children, I was expected to interpret the English

world, to explain . . . bills and drug prescriptions and inquiries from the government. I was supposed to unravel the stock market, argue politics with my parents' friends, raise my brother, console my mother.[7]

That was a heavy burden for a child to bear. So was living in two different worlds. There was the world at home, with a foreign language and customs Americans did not understand. Then there was the world outside, with baseball, hot dogs, and native-born Americans who felt comfortable in their own skins.

Berger and his siblings tried to keep the two worlds separate. They were ashamed of having "parents with coagulated accents who . . . seemed to have an inexhaustible well of grief."[8]

Despite that grief, the Bergers built a life for themselves and their children. They did not become famous or wealthy. Theirs was a workaday existence. They lived, they worked, they struggled to make ends meet. They raised their children.

The Holocaust had marked them, but they did not let it destroy them. In time, Joseph Berger came to appreciate his parents' accomplishment.

They did not forget the past, nor could they overcome it. But they did build a decent life in spite of it. That alone was an impressive achievement.

The Taint
of Evil

The Holocaust became a black mark on Germany's national history. In one way or another, every German had to come to terms with it. Some tried to justify their actions or explain them away. Others simply tried to forget. Only a few openly admitted their wrongs or apologized for them.

For the Allies, sorting out the guilty from the innocent was a huge task. Some considered it an unnecessary one. They favored collective responsibility: holding the Germans as a people accountable for Nazi crimes.

Survivor Simon Wiesenthal and many others called this an injustice. They did not want the guilty to go free, but neither did they want the innocent to be punished.

After World War II, the Allies grappled with whether to hold only the Nazi leaders accountable for the Holocaust, or the whole German nation.

Wiesenthal could not forget that two Nazis had saved his life and helped him get his wife, Cyla, into safe hiding. To him, these men were "living proof that it was possible to survive the Third Reich with clean hands . . . [and] that there is no such thing as collective guilt."[1]

The Search for Vengeance

Many Jews could not dismiss collective guilt so readily. In their eyes, the German nation was stained for all time by crimes so terrible they demanded vengeance.

Soon after the war, squads of militant Jews spread over Europe. These men had fought with an all-Jewish unit under British command. They had done their duty as soldiers. Now they would take their crusade against Nazism a step further.

Their plan was simple: track down and execute SS officers in hiding. They had an eighteen-page list of names. They considered everyone on it to be under sentence of death.

For a young Lithuanian Jew named Abba Kovner, executing war criminals was not enough. He believed in collective responsibility; the whole German nation should be punished. He wanted Germans to die the way Jews had died; senselessly and by the millions.

Kovner organized The Avengers, a group of former ghetto fighters and partisans. Like him, these young Jews were filled with righteous fury at the destruction of their homes, their families—their world: They had lost everything and they wanted somebody to pay.

"The destruction was not around us," Kovner once said. "It was within us. We did not imagine we could return to life, that we had a right to have families, to get up and go to work as if accounts with the Germans had been settled."[2]

Abba Kovner testifies at the trial of Adolf Eichmann in 1961. When he was younger, Kovner organized The Avengers and sought revenge against not just the Nazis, but the entire German nation.

The Avengers first planned to poison the water supply of five major German cities. When that proved impossible, they moved to "Plan B"—the poisoning of Nazi prisoners of war awaiting trial at Nuremberg.

Avenger Lebke Distel got a job at the bakery that made the prisoners' bread. He worked there long enough to learn the routine. Then on the night of April 13, 1946, he smuggled two men and a supply of poison into the bakery.

The poison was tasteless and odorless. The three men brushed it over the cooling loaves and slipped out of the building. The next morning, the bread was delivered as usual.

The results of that action have never been clear. Some reports said that a number of prisoners died. Others mention no deaths at all. On April 22, 1946, the Associated Press reported that 2,238 Nazi prisoners were "taken ill in a mysterious plot against [former Nazis]."[3]

The Avengers and the assassination squads won little support. The Allies wanted justice, not revenge. They meant to reestablish the rule of law in Germany and the rest of Europe. Fair trials for accused war criminals would set an example for all the world.

In Palestine, Yishuv leaders also had a reason to stop Jewish violence. They needed the consent of the United Nations to form a Jewish state. Assassinations and terrorism might tip the UN vote against them.

Denazification

While Jews struggled to found a nation in Palestine, Germans faced a "denazification" program. The Allies wanted to purge every trace of Nazism from German national life.

The Allies felt that the German people should know the crimes committed by their leaders during the Holocaust. Many citizens were forced to view the bodies found at the concentration camps.

After the war ended in 1945, they developed a set of guidelines.

Applying those guidelines would not be easy. At the end of the war, the Allies had divided Germany into four occupation zones. The United States, Britain, France, and the Soviet Union each controlled one of these zones. To make denazification work, all four would have to agree to the guidelines.

All four did agree, but words on paper are one thing; action is another. Each nation applied the guidelines in its own particular way.

For example, the guidelines called for investigations of former Nazis. Anyone with a significant Nazi past was to be banned from public positions. This included government employment as well as elective offices.

Some investigators simply handed out questionnaires about Nazi connections and accepted the answers at face value. They did not have the resources to run background checks on thousands of people. This made lying ridiculously easy.

Each of the four Allied powers had its own standards for enforcing the ban on Nazis in public positions. The Americans were strict, especially in the beginning. The English and the French sometimes compromised because they needed trained people to keep their

The anti-Semitic book *The Poisonous Mushroom* was used by the Nazis to get the children of Germany to form racist views.

sectors running. The Soviets simply cleared anyone who joined the Communist party.

In March 1948, the Soviets dropped the denazification program altogether. It continued for a time in the Western zones, declining gradually until it came to an end in 1954. During denazification, the three Western powers sentenced over 3.4 million former Nazis to some type of punishment.

Screening out Nazi leaders was only part of the denazification process. The Allies also planned to denazify German society. They revoked race laws and other repressive measures, disbanded Nazi organizations, and eliminated "racial science" instruction in the schools.

This was a huge task. Since 1935, German schools had taught "racial science." By order of the Minister of Education, this instruction began with six-year-olds.[4]

The education ministry ordered teachers to work racial instruction into every school subject. For example, a 1935 directive said that "World history is to be portrayed as the history of racially-determined peoples."[5]

Postwar Germany faced an uphill battle to rid itself of racist beliefs. It also had to deal with bombed-out cities and a shattered economy. In addition, the country was divided into two new nations: the Federal Republic of Germany (West Germany), which became a

This poster was a tool used to teach racial science in Nazi Germany. Racial science, also called eugenics, planted the seeds of racism in young German minds. After the war, racial science instruction was stopped in German schools.

democracy, and the German Democratic Republic (East Germany), allied to the Soviet Union.

Germany and Israel

In 1949, an Israeli journalist called upon the nation to "impress hatred of the Germans upon our young children and their descendants." This hatred would not stop with the German nation. It would apply to individuals as well: "if we meet a German in our travels . . . we should spit in his face, or at his feet, so that he not forget."[6]

People who shared this view opposed any contact between Israel and either of the two Germanies. This was true even if that contact could mean millions of dollars in reparations.

Prime Minister David Ben-Gurion and many other Israeli leaders saw things differently. Germany existed. Ignoring that fact would not change anything. Reparations, payments from a defeated nation to offset the costs of war, could boost the Israeli economy.

In addition, West Germany seemed eager to rise above its Nazi past. Unlike East Germany, which accepted no blame for the Holocaust, West Germany was ready to talk. It was time, Ben-Gurion said, for statecraft and negotiation.

On April 19, 1951, two Israelis met secretly with West German Chancellor Konrad Adenauer. They had come to talk about reparation payments. Adenauer was ready to listen.

He acknowledged that no amount of money could repay Jewish suffering or restore Jewish dead. But money could help the living to build new lives. It could help the newborn nation of Israel to prosper and grow. It could show, beyond doubt, that West Germany accepted responsibility for the Holocaust.

On January 7, 1952, the Knesset began to debate relations with Germany. Demonstrators rioted in the streets, protesting any contact with Germany. They shattered store windows, overturned parked cars, lobbed teargas grenades into the Knesset chamber.

The teargas broke up the meeting, forcing legislators to flee the room. The demonstrators thought they had scored a victory, but the Knesset had other ideas. That night, they met in secret to continue their deliberations. Finally, on January 9, 1952, they voted to begin negotiations with West Germany: 61 in favor, 50 against, with 5 abstaining (choosing not to vote).

Konrad Adenauer (left) visited Yad Vashem, a Holocaust remembrance organization, in 1966.

Unfinished Business

Despite the protests, talks between Israel and West Germany went forward. By September 1952, those talks had produced a historic agreement.

Konrad Adenauer acknowledged German guilt for the Holocaust. He pledged reparations of $820 million to the Jewish people. Most of that would go to the Israeli government. The rest was earmarked for Jewish refugee relief in other countries.

The German government partially paid back the surviving Jewish people for stolen property. Above, American general Dwight D. Eisenhower inspects paintings that were stolen by the Germans and hidden in a salt mine.

Germany also agreed to pay damages to individual Holocaust survivors. Over time, thousands of survivors qualified for these pensions, as they were called. In 1954, the West German government paid out $6 million in pensions. By 1961, the total was up to $100 million.

The agreement made it clear that reparations did not lessen German guilt or repay Jewish suffering. The money was simply a partial payment for lost wages and stolen property. On that basis, most survivors claimed the pensions as their due.

By the mid-fifties, World War II and the Holocaust no longer dominated the headlines. The war crimes trials were over; the DP camps almost emptied. Europe was largely rebuilt. The Holocaust seemed to be moving from the headlines to the history books.

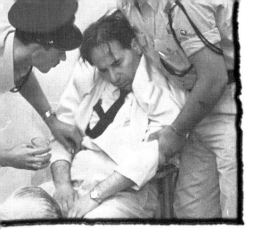

History and Memory

On the twenty-seventh day of the Hebrew month of Nissan (March/April on the civil calendar), sirens all over Israel sound a long blast at exactly 10 A.M. People stop their normal activities: Workers leave their duties, students interrupt their studies, drivers pull to the side of the road and get out of their cars. Everyone stands in silent tribute to the millions who died in the Holocaust.

This is part of *Yom Hashoah*, Holocaust Remembrance Day. Places of entertainment close for the observance. Radio stations play mournful music and recorded testimonies from survivors. Television stations show films about the Holocaust. Newspapers print poems and memorial pieces along with reports about anti-Semitism, Holocaust denial, and other issues facing Israel.

The Knesset, Israel's parliament, established Yom Hashoah as a day of remembrance for Holocaust victims. Israelis mostly ignored it; partly because there were no rituals or customs to mark the day.

Another, deeper, reason had to do with Israel's attitude toward the Holocaust and its victims. In the 1950s, Israel was trying to overcome the image of the Jew as the passive target for gentile hatred.

The Israelis wanted heroes: tough, courageous warriors and nation builders who would never shrink from a fight. Few Holocaust refugees seemed to fit that image. Writer Leah Goldberg called survivors as a group "ugly, impoverished, morally suspect, and hard to love."[1]

A Conspiracy of Silence

According to historian Tom Segev and others, many Israelis who blamed the victims were trying to deal with their own guilt. They had not believed the horrifying reports from Europe during the war. They told themselves that anything so terrible had to be an exaggeration. After the war, brutalized refugees became living proof that the Holocaust was no exaggeration. Rather than face that uncomfortable truth, the Israelis stopped talking about the Holocaust.

Some Holocaust survivors suffered because of this attitude. They needed to tell their stories because the telling helped them work through the pain. Many never got the chance. Others spoke up and came to regret it.

For example, Michael Goldman's most painful memory came from 1943, when he was a seventeen-year-old prisoner in a slave labor camp. Goldman was brought before the camp commandant for some small offense.

The condition of the Holocaust survivors delivered the stark truth to the skeptics of the world about how they had been treated.

The commandant beat him until he fainted. When he regained consciousness, the commandant continued beating him—eighty lashes in all. Goldman was barely alive.

In Israel after the war, Goldman told his story to relatives. They refused to believe him; surely he was exaggerating, they said, or simply mistaken. Such things simply could not happen.

Goldman was crushed. Never had he felt more cut off and alone. "That disbelief was the eighty-first blow," he said later.[2]

The Eighty-First Blow became the title of a film about Goldman's experiences, and a symbol of the disbelief and even hostility that many survivors encountered. Nobody wanted to hear their stories or let them share their pain.

Memory and the Eichmann Trial

On May 23, 1960, Prime Minister David Ben-Gurion made a stunning announcement: Adolf Eichmann, the man who organized and operated the Nazi extermination program, had been captured in Argentina. He was in an Israeli prison, awaiting trial. Israel's silence on the Holocaust was about to end.

For David Ben-Gurion, the importance of Eichmann's trial went beyond the fate of one aging ex-Nazi. Israeli historian Tom Segev pointed out that Ben-Gurion had two goals:

> One was to remind the countries of the world that the Holocaust obligated them to support the only Jewish state on earth. The second was to impress the lessons of the Holocaust on the people of Israel, especially the younger generation.[3]

On the first day of proceedings, Israelis crowded the courtroom to get a look at Eichmann. They expected to see a hard-eyed, swaggering Nazi monster. Instead, they saw a scrawny, aging man with thinning hair and a shabby black suit. Simon Wiesenthal said that Eichmann "looked like a bookkeeper who is afraid to ask for a raise."[4]

When confronted with the charges against him, Eichmann made a startling claim: "I had nothing to do with killing the Jews. I never killed a Jew . . . and I never ordered anybody to kill a Jew."[5]

The statement itself was not nearly as shocking as the fact that it was basically true. Eichmann had never turned on a gas valve to make a "shower room" into a death chamber. He had never shot anybody down, or conducted "selections" to decide who would live and who would die. He was a "desk murderer."

As head of the Gestapo's Department of Jewish Affairs, Eichmann kept the Final Solution running smoothly. Just by issuing an order in Berlin, he could create ghettos

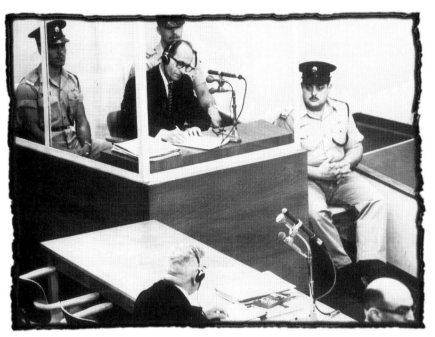

Adolf Eichmann sits in a bulletproof booth and takes notes during his trial.

and fill them with Jews. He could also destroy ghettos and send their inhabitants to work camps or death camps.

In performing these duties, Eichmann created thousands of documents. This mountain of paperwork became evidence in his trial. There was enough of it to destroy Eichmann's claim that he was little more than a clerk, simply carrying out orders.

Though Israeli attorney general Gideon Hausner had this documentation in hand, he planned to use it very little. He had a more ambitious goal: to use the Eichmann case as a

Gideon Hauser was the chief prosecutor for Israel at the trial of Adolf Eichmann.

platform for revealing the full horror of the Holocaust.

He would bring a parade of survivors to the witness stand. Their testimony would show the human cost of Eichmann's memos and letters and requisition forms.

To expose the truth about the Final Solution, Hausner turned the Eichmann trial into more than a simple criminal proceeding. It became a saga, with throngs of reporters and even television cameras. For Eichmann's safety, the Israelis built a booth of bulletproof glass. The image of "the man in the glass booth" made front-page news all over the world.

The trial dredged up painful memories for survivors who testified. There were accusations, denunciations, and angry outbursts. There were tears. One man fainted on the witness stand and had to be carried out of the courtroom.

Gideon Hausner was relentless and thorough. By the time he finished, there could be only one verdict—guilty—and only one sentence—death. Adolf Eichmann was hanged on May 31, 1962.

Memory and Evil

The importance of the Eichmann trial went beyond the fate of one man. It exposed the inner workings of the Nazi "killing machine." In the process, it shocked the world and revived interest in the Holocaust.

In Israel, survivors could finally talk about their experiences. People were willing to listen. By the 1970s, historians and other scholars were studying Holocaust history in detail. They collected survivor testimonies into vast archives and preserved the documentary record for future generations.

Philosopher George Santayana once warned that "Those who cannot remember

Some of the survivors who testified at the Eichmann trial were overcome with emotion. Witness Yehiel Dinur Katzenik was helped by court guards after he fainted during his testimony.

the past are condemned to repeat it."[6] Most Jews would agree with this statement.

Memory is important in Jewish tradition. Memory of a shared history binds the Jewish people together into one community. Memory of the dead honors the lives that they lived. Memory of the Holocaust creates an enduring symbol of human evil.

The slogan "Never Again" has a companion: "Never Forget." Together, they sum up the hope that memory and watchfulness can prevent such horrors in the future.

Memory and Controversy

With a subject as big as the Holocaust, it should not be surprising that people disagree about how it should be remembered. Some consider the Holocaust a Jewish tragedy. Others insist that the term applies equally to non-Jewish victims of the Nazis.

A well-publicized disagreement between Simon Wiesenthal and Elie Wiesel illustrates this issue. Both men were Holocaust survivors with worldwide reputations. Wiesenthal, the "Nazi hunter," devoted his life to bringing Holocaust criminals to justice. Wiesel, winner of the 1986 Nobel Peace Prize, had worked tirelessly to help survivors and support the cause of world peace.

Elie Wiesel delivers a speech in Washington, D.C. Wiesel wrote a gripping account of his concentration camp experience called *Night*.

Wiesel believed that the Holocaust was primarily a Jewish tragedy. Though the Nazis had killed about five million gentiles, he argued that the Final Solution applied only to Jews. He feared that a broader definition of the Holocaust would diminish, or reduce, the Jewish tragedy.

Wiesenthal saw things differently, as he explained to writer Alan Levy: "I was for over four years in different camps with people from fifteen nations: Jews, Gentiles, gypsies, communists. . . . For me was the Holocaust

Simon Wiesenthal considered the Holocaust a "human tragedy," and not solely a Jewish tragedy. Wiesenthal helped bring Adolf Eichmann and other Nazis to justice.

not only a Jewish tragedy, but also a human tragedy."[7]

Jewish tragedy or human tragedy? In the United States, arguments on that question affected the development of the Holocaust Memorial Museum in Washington, D.C., and the Simon Wiesenthal Center for Holocaust Studies in Los Angeles. Both institutions opened in 1993. The museum covered various victim groups, but focused on the Jews. The Wiesenthal Center gave broad coverage to gentile victims of the Nazis. It also looked beyond the Holocaust to deal with broader issues of racism and hatred.

In Israel, the conflict was not about Jewish and gentile victims. It was about using the Holocaust to justify military and political actions.

During his term as Prime Minister, Menachem Begin returned again and again to the Holocaust. For example, he launched a 1981 surprise attack on Palestinian camps in Lebanon by using the name of Treblinka, the extermination center that gassed some 870,000 Jews.

The Israelis had to attack, he said. The alternative was "Treblinka, and we have decided that there will be no more Treblinkas."[8]

When other nations criticized Israel for striking first, Begin brushed them aside. He

Menachem Begin (center) looks on as President Jimmy
Carter delivers a speech on November 1, 1978.

claimed that the Holocaust had forever taken away any nation's right to stand in judgment on Israel.

Some Israelis agreed with Begin. Others supported the action in Lebanon, but disagreed that Israel was beyond moral law. Still others opposed any military strike on principle.

Anti-war Israelis made their feelings known. One Holocaust survivor parked himself at Yad Vashem, Israel's Holocaust Memorial. He began a hunger strike to protest the war itself, and the way Begin used the Holocaust to justify it. The man's name was Shlomo Schmelzman. He had lived through the Warsaw ghetto and the Buchenwald concentration camp. With his credentials as a survivor, he created such a sensation that the Yad Vashem staff evicted him from the grounds.

Shlomo Schmelzman's lonely anti-war crusade is only one example of the gulf between those who lived through the Holocaust and those who did not. Survivors could not just slip back into their old identities, as if nothing had happened. The Holocaust had forever changed them. Their challenge was accepting that and going on in spite of it.

6

Legacy of the Holocaust

In the twenty-first century, the Holocaust will pass from living memory. Somewhere in the world, the last person who actually experienced it will die. There will be no one left to put a human face on the Nazi attempt to wipe out the Jewish people.

This does not mean that the Holocaust will be forgotten. It does mean that it will be remembered in a different way. People will study it as history, and commemorate it with symbols and rituals.

This kind of remembering is not deeply personal. It is standing respectfully when the sirens wail on Yom Hashoah morning, or reading about the horrors of a long-ago world. It is touring a Holocaust museum with a guide who explains the meaning of a striped shirt with a yellow star on the front.

People may be deeply moved by what they see and do, but the feelings will be second-hand. This is not "bad"; it is simply the way of things. Human beings do not experience history in the same way they experience living reality.

The world has been preparing for the time when no living person will have any direct memory of the Holocaust or World War II. Governments and private foundations have built memorials and museums. They have created archives to hold vast collections of photos, documents, and books.

Over seven hundred thousand people each year visit the monument and museum built on the ruins of Auschwitz. Visitors to Amsterdam, Holland, can tour the house where Anne Frank wrote her famous diary. By the turn of the twenty-first century, the United States had over one hundred Holocaust museums and research centers. All had been created since the mid-1980s.

Memory and Denial

Alongside this growth in memorial projects, the Holocaust denial movement took shape. Deniers claim that the Holocaust should not be memorialized at all, because it never happened.

They began to gain notice in 1977, when Northwestern University professor Arthur R. Butz published a book that called the Holocaust a hoax, or fraud. Just two years later, in 1979, The Institute for Historical Review (IHR) in Los Angeles, California, held a convention for Holocaust deniers.

Many of these people rejected the name "Holocaust deniers." They thought of themselves as *revisionists*. They readily acknowledged that Jews as a group suffered horribly during World War II. They disagreed with three points of mainstream Holocaust history:

1. That the Holocaust was a well-organized and efficient program of mass killing.
2. That six million Jews were killed.
3. That the Final Solution was a plan for genocide, complete destruction, of the Jewish people.

In other words, they attacked those features that made the Holocaust a unique event in human history. They argued that there were no gas chambers, no organized extermination programs, no six million Jewish martyrs.

Holocaust deniers dispute the purpose, and even the existence, of gas chambers. The rear view of a gas chamber at Majdanek camp clearly shows how it operated. The furnace on the right created carbon monoxide gas, which was pumped through the pipe and into the chamber. Those inside suffocated to death.

Deniers try to reshape Holocaust history by ignoring some facts and explaining away others. According to them, Jews shipped from ghettos were going to work camps, not gas chambers. Perhaps three hundred thousand Jews died in the camps, say deniers, mainly of disease and starvation.

Some deniers claim that the gas chambers never existed. Others say they were used to disinfect clothes and bedding. Many

Holocaust deniers feel that the Final Solution itself was not a plan for genocide, but only for resettling Jews outside of German lands.

Yad Vashem

Holocaust denial was not an active movement when Israel created its Holocaust museum. The project began in May 1953, when the Knesset formed the Martyrs' and Heroes' Remembrance Authority. The new agency had one task: to create an Israeli Holocaust museum and memorial. *Yad Vashem* (a

The sign at the entrance to the Garden of the Righteous Among Nations is written in Hebrew and English.

Hebrew word meaning "a monument and a name") was the result.

Though Yad Vashem honored the six million victims, it did not focus on them. Instead, it concentrated on heroes: rescuers, ghetto fighters, partisans. Even the path leading up to the building is devoted to heroes.

The path is lined with carob trees. Each tree bears the name of a righteous gentile who helped to rescue Jews from the Nazis. Near the museum entrance is an old fishing boat, once used to transport Danish Jews to safety in neutral Sweden.

Prisoners of the German soldiers await their fate after the Warsaw ghetto uprising. Yad Vashem recognizes the uprising as one of the key examples of courage displayed by the Jewish people during the Holocaust.

Inside the building, the very first exhibit honors the Warsaw ghetto uprising. This image of doomed Jews going down fighting sets the tone for the whole museum.

Though Yad Vashem still focuses on heroes, it has taken a broader view of courage since the Eichmann trial. It honors the quiet courage of parents who comforted their children on the way to the gas chambers, taking the terror out of those last moments of life. It honors the silent defiance of elderly Jews who stood naked and shivering before their killers and did not flinch or look away.

The United States Holocaust Memorial Museum is located at 100 Raoul Wallenberg Place in Washington, D.C. Raoul Wallenberg was a Swedish diplomat who rescued thousands of Jews from the Nazis.

America Remembers the Holocaust

As Yad Vashem presents an Israeli view of the Holocaust, so the United States Holocaust Memorial Museum in Washington, D.C., presents an American one. The museum's permanent exhibit does not begin with brutal Nazis and suffering Jews. It begins with American soldiers liberating the camps.

The theme of liberation begins on the elevators that take visitors to the first exhibit. On the way up, visitors see films of American troops entering concentration and death camps. They hear the recorded voice of an American soldier:

Visitors to the United States Holocaust Memorial Museum view the liberation mural upon their arrival to the beginning of the museum's permanent exhibit.

The patrol leader called in by radio and said that we have come across something that we are not sure what it is. It's a big prison of some kind, and there are people running all over. Sick, dying, starved people. And you take to an American, uh, such a sight as that, you . . . you can't imagine it. You, you just . . . things like that don't happen.[1]

The elevators open and visitors come face-to-face with a gigantic black and white photograph of American soldiers. They are looking down at a pile of half-burned bodies. For a moment, the visitors are part of the scene. They stand opposite the soldiers, sharing their horror.

The original film, recording, and photograph are authentic. Each of them depicts a verified fact. The way these facts are put together produce an emotionally powerful display.

Other exhibits carefully document the facts of the Holocaust, sparing none of the terror and tragedy. Then the permanent display ends as it began—with rescue and redemption. In a room with walls covered in Jerusalem stone, visitors hear the voices of survivors: people who endured the camps and ghettos and went on to build new lives. Their very existence proves that the Final Solution failed.

The striped uniforms of camp prisoners are displayed on the second floor of the United States Holocaust Memorial Museum.

Lessons of the Holocaust

The Nazis did not create an "Aryan master race," wipe the Jewish people off the face of the earth, or even win the war. What they did do was show the terrible cost of racism and hatred.

This is the legacy and the lesson of the Holocaust. It was not some unearthly horror that struck with overwhelming force. It was a process that started small and developed over time. It was not the work of evil monsters with super powers. It was the work of human beings. It was not inevitable, something that could not be stopped. It did not have to happen.

This is perhaps the second-hardest lesson of the Holocaust; that people caused it, so people could have prevented it. They could have said no instead of yes. They could have refused to hate, or to fight, or to march in lockstep with an evil regime. They could have changed the course of history. But they did not.

This is why learning about the Holocaust is so important, and denying it so dangerous. The Holocaust shows that human beings are capable of great evil. Denying that, or ignoring it, will not make the evil go away. Only by confronting it can humankind hope to build a future in which "never again" means exactly what it says.

Timeline

February 14, 1896—Theodor Herzl publishes *The Jewish State*, launching the Zionist movement.

May 7, 1945—Germany surrenders to the Allies. The war in Europe ends.

August 1945—The Allies create a multinational court to judge Nazi war crimes.

October 18, 1945—Nazi leaders are indicted for war crimes.

October 24, 1945—The Charter of the United Nations is approved.

November 20, 1945—First public session of the Nuremberg trial begins.

April. 13, 1946—The Avengers poison bread intended for accused Nazi war criminals in a Nuremberg prison.

June 1946—The United Nations creates its Commission on Human Rights.

October 1, 1946—Nuremberg verdicts read in open court.

October 16, 1946—Nuremberg defendants who were sentenced to death are hanged.

November 29, 1947—The United Nations passed Resolution 181, partitioning Palestine into Jewish and Arab states.

March 1948—Soviets drop the denazification program in their sector. It continues for a time in the Western zones.

May 14, 1948—The new nation of Israel declares its independence.

May 15, 1948—Israel attacked by neighboring countries. War of Independence begins.

December 9, 1948—United Nations ratifies the Convention on the Prevention and Punishment of the Crime of Genocide.

December 10, 1948—United Nations ratifies the Universal Declaration of Human Rights.

January 9, 1952—Israeli Knesset votes to begin negotiations with West Germany.

September 10, 1952—Israel and West Germany sign reparations agreement.

May 23, 1960—Israeli Prime Minister David Ben-Gurion announces capture of Adolf Eichmann.

April 10, 1961—Trial of Adolf Eichmann begins in Israel.

May 31, 1962—Adolf Eichmann is executed.

Chapter Notes

Chapter 1. "Never Again!"

1. Howard M. Sachar, *A History of Israel From the Rise of Zionism to Our Time*, second edition (New York: Alfred A. Knopf, 1996), p. 40.

2. Mark Tessler, *A History of the Israeli-Palestinian Conflict* (Bloomington and Indianapolis: Indiana University Press, 1994), p. 269.

3. "Preamble," The Declaration of Independence.

4. "Universal Declaration of Human Rights," United Nations, <http://www.un.org/Overview/rights.html> (June 1, 2003).

5. Ibid.

Chapter 2. Interrupted Lives

1. David E. Fass, "After Auschwitz—A Trip to Central Europe," *Lamp*, (Rockland, N.Y.: Temple Beth Sholom, March 2001), <http://www.tbs-nc.org/lamp_v16n6.htm> n.d. (May 12, 2002).

2. Simon Wiesenthal, *The Sunflower: On the Possibilities and Limits of Forgiveness* (New York: Schocken Books, 1997), p. 25.

3. Ibid., p. 42.

4. Ibid.

5. Anton Gill, *The Journey Back from Hell: Conversation with Concentration Camp Survivors: An Oral History* (New York: William Morrow and Company, 1988), p. 104.

6. Ibid., p. 167.

Chapter 3. Childhood Lost

1. Anton Gill, *The Journey Back from Hell: Conversation with Concentration Camp Survivors: An Oral History* (New York: William Morrow and Company, 1988), p. 447.

2. Kurt Fuchel, "Kurt Fuchel's Memoirs," *The Kindertransport Association*, <http://www.kindertransport.org/memfuch1.htm> (June 15, 2003).

3. Bloeme Evers-Emden, "Between Two Religions: Happy Forever After?" *The Hidden Child Foundation/ADL*, 2001, <http://www.adl.org/hidden/between_religions/hc_7-1-happy_forever.asp> (June 12, 2003).

4. William H. Donat, "Could I Still Be a Little Catholic Deep Inside: A Dual Experience," *The Hidden Child Foundation/ ADL*, 2003, <http://www.adl.org/hidden/between_religions/hc_7-1-still_catholic.asp> (June 12, 2003).

5. Ibid.

6. Isabella Leitner with Irving A. Leitner, *Saving the Fragments: From Auschwitz to New York* (New York: New American Library, 1985), p. 114.

7. Joseph Berger, *Displaced Persons: Growing up American After the Holocaust* (New York: Scribner, 2001), p. 18.

8. Ibid., p. 17.

Chapter 4. The Taint of Evil

1. Simon Wiesenthal, *Justice Not Vengeance* (New York: Grove Weidenfeld, 1989), p. 10.

2. Rich Cohen, *The Avengers: A Jewish War Story* (New York: Alfred A. Knopf, 2000), p. 191.

3. Ibid., p. 212.

4. George L. Mosse, *Nazi Culture: Intellectual, Cultural, and Social Life in the Third Reich* (New York: Schocken Books, 1966), pp. 283–284.

5. Ibid., p. 284.

6. Tom Segev, *The Seventh Million: The Israelis and the Holocaust* (New York: Hill and Wang, 1993), p. 190.

Chapter 5. History and Memory

1. Tom Segev, *The Seventh Million: The Israelis and the Holocaust* (New York: Hill and Wang, 1993), p. 179.

2. Ibid., p. 155.

3. Ibid., p. 327.

4. Alan Levy, *The Wiesenthal File* (Grand Rapids, Mich.: William B. Eerdmans Publishing Company, 1993), p. 135.

5. John Weiss, *Ideology of Death: Why the Holocaust Happened in Germany* (Chicago: Ivan R. Dee, 1996), p. 380.

6. WHAT IS HISTORY? <http://www.unf.edu/~clifford/craft/what.htm> (June 3, 2002).

7. Levy, p. 435.

8. Segev, p. 399.

Chapter 6. Legacy of the Holocaust

1. Tim Cole, *Selling the Holocaust: From Auschwitz to Schindler How History is Bought, Packaged, and Sold* (New York: Routledge, 1999), p. 152.

Glossary

Allies—During World War II, the group of nations headed by Great Britain and later joined by the United States and the Soviet Union.

anti-Semitism—Hatred of, or discrimination against, Jews as a group.

Aryan—Nazi term for Nordic, or Northern European, peoples.

Avengers—A paramilitary group of Jews who sought vengeance against former Nazis after the war.

Axis—During World War II, the group of nations headed by Germany, opposing the Allies.

Brecha (Hebrew: "to smuggle")—An illegal operation to get Jews into Palestine in defiance of British immigration quotas.

collective responsibility—The idea that all members of a group are responsible for the actions of their leaders.

concentration camp syndrome—A term once used to describe the mental and physical problems afflicting concentration camp survivors. Later included with similar disorders under "post-traumatic stress disorder."

denazification—Allied program to exclude former Nazis from government positions and eliminate Nazi programs from German society.

Department of Jewish Affairs—SS agency headed by Adolf Eichmann, who was eventually charged with carrying out the Nazis' Final Solution for Jews.

displaced persons (DP) camps—Temporary shelters where Holocaust survivors could receive food, lodging, medical care, and other necessities.

Final Solution—The term applied to Nazi plans to exterminate the Jewish people.

flashback—A memory so vivid that the original incident seems to be happening over again. Common in post-traumatic stress disorder.

genocide—The systematic extermination, or attempted extermination, of an entire racial, ethnic, political, or religious group.

ghetto—During World War II, a run-down neighborhood in which all Jews of an area were forced to live.

Holocaust—Originally, an all-consuming fire. Now used to describe the extermination of more than eleven million people, including six million Jews.

Holocaust denial—The contention that the Holocaust did not happen, or has been greatly exaggerated to gain sympathy for Jewish causes.

jurisdiction—Power and authority over a particular region.

Kindertransport—Before the war, a British program to rescue Jewish children from Germany and Central Europe.

living memory—After an event, the span of time during which eyewitnesses are alive.

Palestine—A region in the Middle East, presently occupied by the modern nation of Israel and the West Bank area along the Jordan River.

post-traumatic stress disorder (PTSD)—A set of symptoms affecting survivors of brutal, life-threatening situations such as combat, terrorism, or imprisonment under inhuman conditions.

reparation—Compensation paid for damage or injury inflicted during a war.

selections—During the Holocaust, a process of choosing prisoners for immediate execution.

sovereign—A self-governing state or nation.

Yishuv—The Jewish community in Palestine, before the founding of Israel.

Yom Hashoah—Holocaust Remembrance Day. On the Hebrew calendar, the twenty-seventh day of Nissan (April/May on the civil calendar).

Further Reading

Appleman-Jurman, Alicia. *Alicia: My Story.* New York: Bantam Books, 1990.

Bachrach, Susan D. *Tell Them We Remember: The Story of the Holocaust.* Washington, D.C.: United States Holocaust Memorial Museum, 1999.

Byers Abells, Chana. *The Children We Remember: Photographs from the Archives of Yad Vashem, the Holocaust Martyrs' and Heroes' Remembrance Authority.* New York: Kar-Ben Publishing, 1983.

Byers, Ann. *The Holocaust Overview.* Springfield, N.J.: Enslow Publishers, Inc., 1998.

Gottfried, Ted. *Displaced Persons: Growing Up American After the Holocaust.* Brookfield, Conn.: Twenty First Century Books, 2001.

Nieuwsma, Milton J. *Kinderlager: An Oral History of Young Holocaust Survivors.* New York: Holiday House, 1998.

Richman, Sophia. *A Wolf in the Attic: The Legacy of a Hidden Child of the Holocaust.* Binghamton, N.Y.: Haworth Press, 2002.

Internet Addresses

Cybrary of the Holocaust
http://remember.org

Simon Wiesenthal Center
http://www.wiesenthal.com/

United States Holocaust Memorial Museum
http://www.ushmm.org/

Yad Vashem: The Holocaust Martyrs' and Heroes' Remembrance Authority
http://www.yad-vashem.org.il/

Index